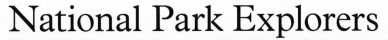

National Park Explorers

GREAT SMOKY MOUNTAINS

by Sara Gilbert

CREATIVE EDUCATION • CREATIVE PAPERBACKS

TABLE OF CONTENTS

Water rushes in Roaring Fork mountain stream.

WELCOME TO GREAT SMOKY MOUNTAINS NATIONAL PARK!

Can you see through all the fog? A bear hunts for berries. An owl sits on a branch. Keep looking. You might find lots of things!

5

The Great Smoky Mountains are named for the fog. In 1934, the area became a national park. The park is on the **border** of North Carolina and Tennessee.

★ *Great Smoky Mountains National Park*
■ *North Carolina*
■ *Tennessee*

View from Clingmans Dome (above); a foggy morning (right)

ANCIENT MOUNTAINS

The Great Smoky Mountains are more than 200 million years old. They are among the oldest mountains on Earth! Some of them are taller than 6,000 feet (1,829 m).

People like to hike up and down the trails in the park. The **Appalachian Trail** runs through Great Smoky.

A white-tailed deer (above); Laurel Falls (right)

KEEP
COUNTING!

Many plants and animals are found in the park. About 1,500 black bears live in Great Smoky. It is also known as the "**Salamander** Capital of the World." At least 30 kinds of salamanders live there.

In the spring and summer, wildflowers bloom. The leaves turn red, orange, and yellow in the fall.

Black-eyed Susan (above); fall colors (right)

POPULAR PEAKS

More than 9 million people visit Great Smoky every year. You can hike, fish, and ride your bike. Some people ride horses.

17

There are lots of **historic** buildings in the park. You can visit a school that was built more than 100 years ago.

Little Greenbrier School, built 1882

18

You can drive through the park, too. The roads are curvy and steep. Be sure to look out your window. The mountains are beautiful, even if it is foggy!

Park visitors can explore many different places.

Activity

FOG IT UP

Materials needed:
Glass jar
Kitchen strainer
Hot water
Ice cubes

Step 1: Fill the jar with hot water. Let it sit for about a minute.

Step 2: Pour out almost all the water. Leave about one inch (2.5 cm) in the jar.

Step 3: Put the strainer over the top of the jar.

Step 4: Place three or four ice cubes in the strainer.

Step 5: Watch what happens when the cold and warm air mix!

Glossary

Appalachian Trail — a 2,185-mile (3,516 km) hiking trail in the eastern United States

border — the edge of a state

historic — important to the past

salamander — an animal that looks like a lizard and can live on land and in water

Read More

McHugh, Erin. *National Parks: A Kid's Guide to America's Parks, Monuments, and Landmarks.* New York: Black Dog & Leventhal, 2012.

National Geographic. *National Geographic Kids National Parks Guide U.S.A.: The Most Amazing Sights, Scenes, and Cool Activities from Coast to Coast.* Washington, D.C.: National Geographic Society, 2012.

Websites

Kids Discover: National Parks
http://www.kidsdiscover.com/spotlight/national-parks-for-kids/
See pictures from the parks and learn more about their history.

WebRangers
http://www.nps.gov/webrangers/
Visit the National Park Service's site for kids to find fun activities.

Index

Published by Creative Education and Creative Paperbacks
P.O. Box 227, Mankato, Minnesota 56002 • Creative Education
and Creative Paperbacks are imprints of The Creative Company
www.thecreativecompany.us

Design and production by Christine Vanderbeek
Art direction by Rita Marshall
Printed in the United States of America

Photographs by Alamy (Backyard Productions, Pat & Chuck
Blackley, Daniel Dempster Photography, David Dobbs, Michael
Hare), Corbis (145/Jerry Whaley/Ocean, Gary W. Carter, Karen
Kasmauski/Science Faction, Joe McDonald), Dreamstime
(Wisconsinart), Getty Images (Kick Images), Shutterstock (33333,
S1001, Tarchyshnik Andrei, Matt Antonino, Natalia Bratslavsky,
Tony Campbell, cristi180884, IrinaK, jadimages, Sergiy Kuzmin,
Geir Olav Lyngfjell, Tim Mainiero, Nagel Photography, RTimages,
Mike Truchon, Jerry Whaley, zokru)

Library of Congress Cataloging-in-Publication Data
Gilbert, Sara. • Great Smoky Mountains / by Sara Gilbert. • p. cm.
— (National park explorers) • *Summary*: A young explorer's
introduction to Great Smoky Mountains National Park, covering
its mountain landscape, plants, animals such as salamanders, and
activities such as horseback riding. • Includes index. • ISBN 978-1-
60818-633-4 (hardcover) • ISBN 978-1-62832-241-5 (pbk) • ISBN
978-1-56660-670-7 (eBook) • 1. Great Smoky Mountains (N.C. and
Tenn.)—Juvenile literature. I. Title.

F443.G7G55 2016
976.8'89—dc23   2014048726

CCSS: RI.1.1, 2, 3, 4, 5, 6, 7, 10; RI.2.1, 2, 3, 5, 6, 7; RI.3.1, 3, 5, 7;
RF.1.1, 3, 4; RF.2.4

First Edition HC 9 8 7 6 5 4 3 2 1
First Edition PBK 9 8 7 6 5 4 3 2 1